Angela Rippon's
Learn with
Victoria Plum
FLOWERS

Purnell

It seems like magic—there's something flowering all the year round! Even in the winter there is a flower to brighten up a grey day.

The ground may be covered in snow, but this won't stop the *snowdrop* from peeping up through the soil and opening its delicate petals . . .

. . . and the *winter aconite*, along with the *lesser celandine*, will also be showing themselves. To tell them apart, the *lesser celandine* has star-like flowers, while the *winter aconite* is more like a buttercup in shape.

Wherever you live, be it town or country, you'll find the *ragwort*. Its chief flowering season is late summer to autumn, but it's here on the winter page because it has been known to flower at Christmas . . . and any flower that can do that deserves a special mention!

Now it's springtime—and as the weather brightens up, so does the countryside!

Wild daffodils are smaller than those grown in gardens, but they are just as pretty. You'll probably find several plants all growing together.

In hedges and bushy places, the *greater stitchwort* creeps around. Its tiny white flowers are like stars.

The *primrose* is one of the most popular spring flowers, growing in woods and on banks.

The *sweet violet* likes a grassy bank to grow on, where it can hide itself among other plants. Its little flowers are well worth looking out for.

The *cowslip* comes into flower year after year, with only a tiny spot of yellow colour at the drooping end of each funnel-shaped flowerhead. Each plant looks like a bunch, all by itself!

In summertime, there are all kinds of flowers out, wherever you look! Here's a flower which everyone knows— the *buttercup*. And, of course, the *daisy*! This is the commonest sort of wild flower, although there is more than one kind of daisy. It's found in lawns as well as in meadows and woodland. At night and in wet weather the petals close up.

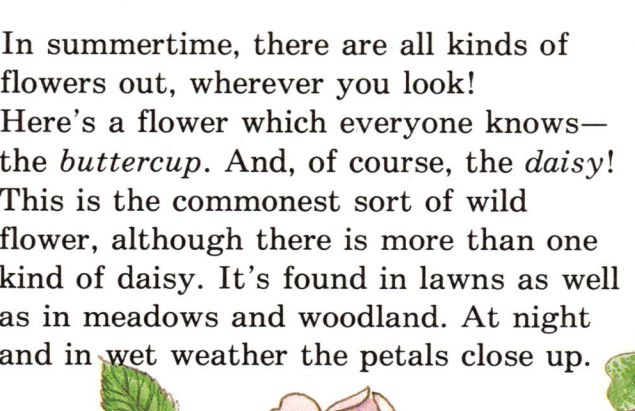

The pretty *dog rose* flowers on bushes or trees, which grow scarlet fruit called *hips* in autumn. *Rose hip syrup* is made from these.

Spotted orchid is a beautiful flowering plant. The flower is made up of light purple blooms in a single, tapering flowerhead. Have you ever seen a *red poppy* in a cornfield? It's a very striking flower. Another poppy to look out for is the *Welsh poppy*, which has a yellow flower.

As autumn comes many of the summer-flowering plants are still blooming, and will do so until the first frosts arrive.

One of the brightest of the autumn flowers is the *autumn crocus*, which blooms in meadowland all over the country.

In the cornfield the tiny *scarlet pimpernel* creeps along the ground.

Some types of *wild honeysuckle* bloom in the autumn, bringing scent and colour to the hedgerows.

The *wild teasel* can be seen a long way off—it stands tall and proud, showing off its spiky head.

Did you know that the *ivy* flowers? Autumn is the time to look for it. Although most people use ivy for its leaves, it has clusters of yellowy-green flowers in autumn.

Here is the *bud* of a poppy. See the spiky bits? They are there to protect the flower, and are called *sepals*.

First the *sepals* open, and then the *petals* of the flower. In the centre of the flowers are the *stamens*, which hold pollen, and the *pistil*, where the seeds will grow.

Bees visiting the flower, collect pollen from the stamens. This brushes on to the next flower's pistil, and seeds can begin to form. Eventually, the seed case becomes dry and hard, then breaks up so that the seeds fall to the ground and grow into new plants.

People and plants have been linked together through the centuries. Plants may very well live without people—but people need plants of all kinds!

Girls like to see if their boyfriends are true to them by pulling the petals from a *daisy* one by one, saying 'he loves me, he loves me not' as they do so. There's no guarantee that it works, but it's fun to do! And when you're fed up with that, you can make a daisy chain.

Sugar Plum's written down how to do this in her diary . . .

Pick a daisy with a nice stout stalk.

Make a slit in the stalk with your finger-nail!

Thread the stalk of another daisy through this slit.

Keep doing this until your chain is as long as you want it.

Join up the chain by making a very long slit in the last daisy stalk and poking the head of the first daisy through it.

Nettle and dock

OUCH! THAT NETTLE STUNG ME!

DON'T WORRY; I'VE GOT JUST THE THING. IT'S NOT MAGIC — AT LEAST, NOT MINE! I'LL RUB THIS DOCK LEAF ON THE NETTLE STING.

THAT'S BETTER, VICTORIA!

ALWAYS LOOK AROUND FOR A DOCK LEAF WHEN A NETTLE STINGS YOU, AND RUB IT ON THE STING. YOU'RE SURE TO FIND ONE, BECAUSE THE TWO PLANTS USUALLY GROW IN THE SAME PLACE.

Another thing to do for fun is to make a *dandelion clock*. You'll need a dandelion flower that has gone to seed and looks like this . . .

Pick it and gently puff at it—and at each puff, say 'One o'clock' then 'Two o'clock' and so on, until there are no more fluffy bits to puff at. Then you *should* know what time it is!

Shyly tucked away under larger plants, the violet's sweet scent is one of Victoria's favourites. They are found in woods and shady places in the Spring.

The wild Arum is another plant found in woods. Also called Lords and Ladies, the plant has dark spots on its leaves. The name comes from the time when rich people covered up blemishes like moles with black beauty spots!

Fields and meadows

Out beyond the Great Wood there are lots of bright, sunny meadows where wild flowers thrive. Victoria loves to walk among them when she's out and about. Here are some of the ones that she often finds. Look out for them yourself next time you go out to a meadow.

Red Clover
smells so
sweet!

Wild Pansy
has a tiny
flower which
may be yellow,
purple, or a
mixture of
both

**Creeping
buttercup**
can spread
across a whole
field, making
it look yellow
all over.

Meadowsweet
has another name
too — 'queen of
the meadows'.

Not all plants grow well in the same place. Some plants actually prefer very dry soil, while others will only be happy in really wet, sticky soil. The temperature of the place is important, too.

Pond and marsh

The wetter the soil the more chance there is of finding lots of different plants. But mind you don't get your feet wet—look, Victoria has found herself in a really soggy place!

Common valerian has a pretty flower-head — but a horrible smell.

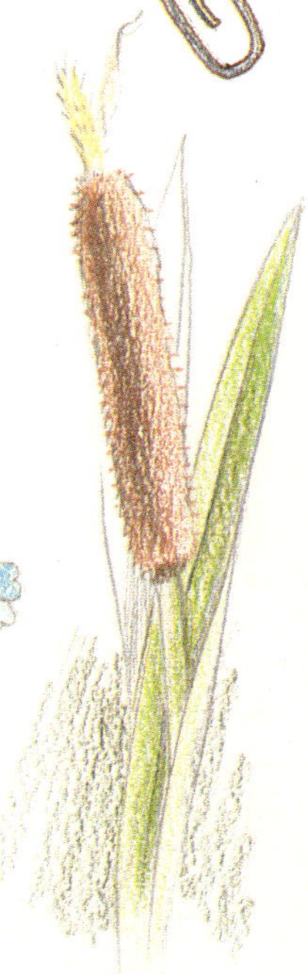

Forget-me-not is a plant which grows in many gardens, but it has a 'wet' variety, too.

Reed mace are often called bulrushes.

Marsh marigold brightens up most damp places.

Victoria's lucky. She can fly over this sort of wet ground; but ordinary people cannot do this—so be careful. Water can be dangerous—and it is better to keep your feet on dry land. Don't go to marshy places unless it is with a sensible grown-up, and, even then, take care!

HELLO! WE'RE AT THE SEASIDE FOR THE DAY—AND I'VE LEFT BEN AND SUGAR PLUM HAVING A PICNIC ON THE SAND DUNES SO THAT I CAN SHOW YOU SOME OF THE PLANTS WHICH BRIGHTEN UP THE SEASHORE. THEY NEED TO BE VERY STURDY TO FACE THE WIND, STORMS AND SALT FROM THE SEA, ESPECIALLY UP HERE ON THIS CLIFF!

Grasses such as *lyme grass*, *marram grass* and *couch grass* help to make a base for flowering plants to survive in. Without them, the soil would simply slide away.

Sea
lavender

Sea
plantain

Sea
aster

Sea
purslane

Where the marsh meets the sea, these plants love to grow. Although they are marsh plants they prefer the seaside.

I JUST LOVE THESE CLIFFSIDE PLANTS, DON'T YOU? LOOK AT THEM WITH ME, BUT DON'T GO NEAR THE EDGE WHEN YOU'RE OUT AT THE SEASIDE YOURSELF. I'D HATE YOU TO HAVE ANY ACCIDENTS! AND NEVER, NEVER CLIMB A CLIFF—THERE COULD BE A LANDSLIDE.

On the sand dunes, among the grasses, there are some different plants.

Sea spurry

Thrift

Sea campion

Sea rocket draws water from deep down in the ground, through a long taproot.

Viper's bugloss has lots of hairs all over it to save water and shield the plants from the sun.

On the beach, the sea pea needs strong roots to stop it getting shifted by the pounding sea.

Nature's helpers

In order to produce flowers and seeds, plants need help from other things in Nature—just look at all the help they get!

Firstly, insects help plants by carrying pollen from one plant to another. To attract insects to their nectar, some plants have flowers with a lovely smell, bright petals and even, sometimes, lines or spots to guide the visitors inside them.

Not all plants need the help of insects to spread their pollen. Grass flowers have no petals; their pollen is easily blown off them by the wind.

Flowers produce lots and lots of seeds—far more than they need. Only a very few manage to grow into new plants—the rest get eaten by little creatures, or fail to find a nice patch of soil, or get caught in very cold weather.

When a plant has produced seeds, the seeds than have to find a suitable growing place. The wind often helps to take the seeds far away. Here's the seed of a sycamore, with 'wings' to help it fly.

Animals such as squirrels, collecting food for their winter stores, often drop seeds. These may grow into new plants. Birds drop seeds, too.

Some seeds float. All wrapped up in a cocoon-like pod, the seeds of the *sea rocket* are washed along the shore.

Some seeds have hooks which catch on the coats of passing animals, or humans! When it brushes off later, it will grow in a distant spot away from its parent.

One way you can keep wild flowers growing is to collect some seed for yourself, or buy a packet of wild flower seeds, and plant them in a garden or on a bank.

Mind out!

Some plants look very pretty, but are very dangerous for people to touch. Read this page carefully, and stay away from the plants shown on it, because even Victoria's magic won't help you if you don't!

JUST TOUCHING THESE PLANTS CAN BE DANGEROUS, BECAUSE IF, BY ACCIDENT, YOUR FINGERS STRAY TO YOUR MOUTH, YOU COULD SWALLOW THE POISON.

The **fox-glove** produces a nasty poison.

The leaves and seeds of **yew trees** are deadly poisonous.

Hemlock grows by the roadside, but it is so poisonous that you could get very ill from it.

The **deadly nightshade** has purple bell-like flowers and black berries. It is a very dangerous plant.

The **wild arum** is called **lords and ladies**, and it's really poisonous too, although it looks pretty.

And it's not just flowers! Lots of toadstools are poisonous. Never eat anything you find—the difference between a toadstool or mushroom that is poisonous, and one that isn't, can't be easily seen.

How to press flowers

I *NEVER* PICK A WILD FLOWER UNLESS I CAN SEE FOR MYSELF THAT THERE ARE LOTS AND LOTS OF OTHERS JUST LIKE IT, SO THAT ONE FLOWER WON'T BE MISSED. YOU NEVER KNOW — IF I WERE TO PICK THE ONLY ONE I COULD FIND, THAT SORT OF FLOWER MIGHT NOT BE FOUND THERE AGAIN!

Lay the flowers carefully on a piece of kitchen roll paper, and spread out the leaves and petals so that they lie flat and do not touch each other.

Put another piece of kitchen roll paper on top, and place some heavy books on top of that.

YOU CAN PRESS SEAWEED, TOO!

Forget all about it for three weeks, and then . . . Peep and see! Your flowers should be dry, and stiff. They'll be brittle, too, so you must be careful with them.

AT OTHER TIMES I JUST PAINT THE FLOWERS WITH MY BRUSH AND PAINTBOX. THAT WAY, I DON'T HAVE TO PICK THEM. I PAINT THEM IN MY FLOWER DIARY— SEE, HERE IT IS, WITH A PAGE FOR EACH MONTH OF THE YEAR (IT WAS JUST AN ORDINARY EXERCISE BOOK TO BEGIN WITH!). I USE A VERY FINE BRUSH SO THAT I CAN PAINT THE THIN PARTS EASILY—AND I MAKE SURE A PAGE IS DRY BEFORE I SHUT THE BOOK. OH YES—AND I ALWAYS WRITE THE DATE WHEN I SAW THE FLOWER UNDER EACH PICTURE AND LABEL IT SO THAT I KNOW WHAT IT IS AND WHERE IT'S GROWING. IT'S SURPRISING HOW MANY DIFFERENT TYPES OF FLOWER I'VE COLLECTED IN THIS WAY.

AUGUST

Scarlet Pimpernel

Dog Rose

Ground Elder

Bindweed

If you're keen to find out more about wild flowers, there will be lots of books about them at your local library. If you don't know how to find the right books get the librarian to help you.

And if your birthday, or Christmas, is approaching, ask for a good guide book such as *Purnell's Spot and Stick: Wild Flowers* or *The Observer's Book of Wild Flowers*.